G000136094

iill

E

e

War diary of John Gill

 England

In the Blue - Behind the Front Line

This book is a transcript of a young man's diary throughout World War 2. It is a personal interpretation of events at the time and does not necessarily represent opinions or values of the writer. Whilst efforts have been made to clarify some events and terminology neither the author nor the publisher guarantee the accuracy of events, places or dates in this transcript or accompanying text.

First edition

ISBN 978-1-9998266-4-2

Graphic design by Chris Gill for MC World Enterprise

Published by IVANA INTERNATIONAL, England

TABLE OF CONTENTS

In the Blue - Behind the Front Line

IN THE BLUE

Behind the Front Line

Prepared by Linda & Chris
...so that one small story amongst the many will not be forgotten

In the Blue - Behind the Front Line

1. THE PROLOGUE

It was November 1921, a month in which Albert Einstein was awarded the Nobel Prize in Physics and hyperinflation in Germany meant that there were 263 German Marks to one US Dollar. It was an unremarkable month in an unremarkable year, but on Sunday, 27th November of this year John Gill was born. He was the second child of three born to Alice May Gill.

The Gill family was not wealthy, John's father died when he was quite young and the family as a whole, like so many others, had suffered its share of hardship throughout a difficult period in history. In his adult life John spoke little of his early years but did mention attending an "Open Air School" in Balby *(Note: Open air schools were quite common in 1920-30s since fresh air and good ventilation were thought to reduce the risks of tuberculosis which was rife in this era.)*, but for a lot of his childhood the family lived in Edenthorpe, a village just east of Doncaster.

By the time John joined the forces the family home was a small red brick terraced house in St Mary's Road, Doncaster which John shared with grandfather, mother, younger brother Frank and older sister Mary (In his letters home John refers to No. "91", this being the number of the house he called home). His mother stayed in this house until the late 1970s.

The driving force that kept the family together was without doubt John's mother. Despite her diminutive stature Alice May Gill was a strong, hard-working woman who worked tirelessly well into old age. She did a variety of jobs and took in lodgers to help support the family before acquiring a small stall in Doncaster mar-

2

ket selling household trinkets, she maintained this stall until retirement. Even into her 90s she was volunteering with the Salvation Army to help "the old people" as she would describe them.

As a teenager John began working as a lorry driver's mate, he would travel around the country collecting or delivering a variety of goods, but mainly timber or paper. In his spare time at home he would help his grandfather with his hobby and part-time business of breeding, showing and selling budgerigars. In the evening he would frequently visit the local YMCA or cinema. The stability brought about by his mother's efforts meant that life for the family was homely and comfortable as the siblings approached and entered adulthood. But, in 1939 life would be disrupted and it would never be the same again.

FOLLOWING A SERIES OF NEWSPAPER ARTICLES ABOUT THE WAR WITH GERMANY IN 1914, H. G. WELLS PUBLISHED A BOOK TITLED "THE WAR THAT WILL END WAR". HE WAS OF COURSE REFERRING TO WW1 AND THREE YEARS LATER THE PHRASE WAS MADE FAMOUS WHEN WOODROW WILSON USED IT IN A SPEECH TO THE US CONGRESS. IN THAT WAR UP TO 10 MILLION PEOPLE LOST THEIR LIVES ON THE BATTLE FIELDS AND IT SEEMED INCONCEIVABLE THAT LESSONS WOULD NOT BE LEARNED. YET DESPITE THE ENDING OF WW1 IN 1918 IT BECAME CLEAR THAT CONFLICT WITH GERMANY WAS AGAIN GOING TO INTERRUPT THE LIVES OF NOT ONLY JOHN'S FAMILY BUT THE LIVES OF EVERYONE IN BRITAIN AND MANY IN OTHER NATIONS TOO.

Perhaps it was the anticipation of the ensuing war or perhaps they were just the thoughts of a maturing young man coming to terms with himself that caused John to make a few seemingly random entries in an early diary. Though somewhat disjointed and not dated these entries are nevertheless of interest in that they give some insight into the man, his thoughts, and the times in which he grew up:

I remember once when I was going to school with Frank I was trying to show off, jumping the wire fence round the field, of course, I didn't quite make it, I got my legs twisted in the wire and was flying forward on my face. I was badly shaken up but not damaged. My brother for whom I have a very great affection, picked ..... but how can I put it in words.... I can only say that the way he treated me the rest of that day made me double my affection for him. We were very young.

Another memory which has made me curse myself many times, and does not put me in a very good light was still when we were very young. Something turned up, I forget what, but something that made me angry enough to hit my brother, naturally he hit back. Half a dozen of my pals goaded me to give him a hiding (I was by far the biggest). The devil came out in me, and I gave him a hiding, a thing which I shall never forget, or for which I shall never forgive myself. It seems a small thing in writing, but it has left a nasty and lasting taste in my mouth.

My happiest early memories are of Edenthorpe and my school-days, romping through the fields, climbing trees, bird nesting, mushrooming, hide-and-seek in the woods, the boys club in the old hall, that was the best of all. I

4

think it was the club that put a rosy light over the whole district for me. I became abnormally enthusiastic over gymnastics. I became rather good at it and it did me an enormous amount of good. We gave one or two displays, and I was quite proud of myself. I remember one thing my mother told me, "if you are really and genuinely proud of yourself, it doesn't matter a damn what other people think" (not exactly in those words, but that's the general idea). I thought it was a wise remark.

During the latter part of my school-days I think I fell in love with a different girl every day. Something about this girl's mouth, or another's eyes, or that little turned up nose, attracted me. I was a stupid fellow when I was young. The day I always looked passionately forward to was Sunday, we always had a really slap-up feed, but the highlight of Sunday was the arrival of the Beltons. They came every week and Mr Belton had a different story (of the last war) every time. We sat for hours over tea listening to him, he was, or rather is, a first class chap, not really brainy, but the most reliable man I've ever met. He is rather good at most trades, he did wonders for our garden and has wired our house up for electricity (no small job) and has painted our house out more than once.

Another little thing about my brother and that I regret, a small thing but to me important. We shared a bed in our small house and at night, I used to be a most bad-tempered devil, once I got to bed I made him, yes physically made him, keep still. If I was in a really bad mood (which was not infrequent) and he moved when I was on the point of sleep, I would give him a hefty clout. I've done it more than once and I'm heartily ashamed of it.

5

My sister Mary has fought several battles for me, nearly two years older than me, and she has three time as much nerve in some things. The bullies of the village always had an eye on me, perhaps because I didn't follow them around like the rest of the sheep, anyway one chap in particular used to like knocking me around, and my sister has set into him more than once, she did it well too, never failed.

These thoughts, events and actions in John's early life clearly had an emotional impact as he embarked on the journey of adult life under exceptional circumstances that we all hope will never be repeated in our or our children's lifetimes.

Brother - Frank

John

Sibling photographs taken
before demob in 1946 by a
local photographer at Sun-Rae
Studio, 70 Balby Road,
Doncaster.

Sister - Mary

Father

Mother

1947 John Gill and
Elizabeth Joan
Crawshaw are married
at St Georges Church,
Doncaster

8

In the Blue - Behind the Front Line

2. THE WAR BEGINS

On 1st September 1939 German forces invaded Poland, two days later on the 3rd September 1939 Britain and France declared war on Germany. World War II had begun, John was just 17 years old.

At the outset no one new how the war would evolve or for how long it would continue, unlike Germany the allied forces were unprepared for war and there was a great deal of uncertainty. By mid-May 1940 Germany had started land operations in Western Europe and within 6 weeks had invaded and conquered France, Belgium, Luxembourg and the Netherlands. France Surrendered on June 22, 1940 with the French government signing an armistice with Nazi Germany.

At the beginning of the war there was no conscription in Britain and the armed services relied on volunteers. The government quickly realised that this would not provide sufficient forces during the ensuing war and so in October 1939 it was announced that all men aged between 18 and 41 (except for certain "reserved occupations") could be called to join the armed services if required. Conscription was by age and in October 1939 men aged between 20 and 23 were required to register to serve in one of the armed forces.

John's only close experience of the war so far was to see the barrage balloons protecting Manchester's skies when, as a driver's mate he made an overnight stay in the city. There will have been many reports of bombings on the news but seeing something first-hand must have been a stark reminder that the war was not just something to be fought overseas but something that could eventually be fought on the streets of his own home town.

Italy entered the war on 10th June 1940. With the conflict now moving further afield and ever expanding John, now 18 years old, volunteered rather than waiting for conscription. He signed on with the RAF, but having very little experience, like so many young men in times of war, he would be trained and learn the necessary skills while serving in his unit.

Many accounts of wartime experiences are about battles, heroism and conflict, this little book is not that, it is simply one young man's diary. He started out with so much enthusiasm and excitement to document what he probably imagined, despite the obvious dangers, to be an adventure. None of us can totally imagine the horrors of war without having experienced it, and youth can often lead to a degree of naivety especially in that era before mass media and modern systems of communication. John's enthusiasm did not last and as the war progressed he suffered an illness brought on by the living conditions rather than the enemy, but in wars the living conditions themselves can be as much the enemy as the opposing army.

Much of John's war was spent in the "Western Dessert", it might seem strange now but in WW2 British soldiers referred to this desert of North Africa as the "**Blue**". This extract from "The Fighting Tykes: An Informal History of the Yorkshire Regiments in the Second World War" by Charles Whiting & Eric Taylor describes the conditions in the "Blue" if not the unlikely sobriquet:

"'Up the blue' the squaddies of the British Eighth Army called it. From Cairo after they first arrived in Egypt

*they went 'up the blue'; and when they returned more of-
ten than not they were broken men, both in spirit and
body. For two years now the British had been making
confident advances westward through the 'blue' driving
all before them until the steam went out of the advance,
and they would be forced back the way they had come in
what was known cynically as the 'Benghazi Handicap.'
Officially this featureless, arid waste was known as the
Western Desert, stretching from Egypt across the top of
Africa to Libya. But there nothing of Beau Geste roman-
ticism about the Western Desert. The 'blue' was an ex-
panse of flat saltbush, grey earth and yellow rock,
burningly hot and thick with flies by midday and freez-
ingly cold at night. But to some people back in Britain it
was a wonderful place to fight a war. It was a long way
away, it didn't involve them, as a battle in Europe might
have done, and it allowed them to get on with their
lives."*

John was posted to 31 Air Stores Park (31ASP) behind
the front line, and rather than confronting the enemy his
unit would dodge them in order to continue maintaining
support to the vehicles and fighting machines on the
front line. It was not without its dangers but it did leave
time for occasional relaxation. Being a young man on
his first ever trip beyond the shores of his home country
John made good use of these opportunities and writes
more about these than of his war work. Indeed, at one
point he refers to his work as "uninteresting", but it
would have been nice to hear more about it.

However, this is largely a simple transcript of John Gill's
wartime diary. War affects so many lives in different
ways and armies consist of many elements which com-
bine to enable a unified fighting force. This is a story

like many thousands of others that rarely get recorded, a story from behind the allied front line, a story not of fighting but about life. The diary is sometimes disjointed and certainly towards the end becomes sparse. But in the latter days of the war in Europe there must have been other priorities and things to occupy a young man's time that were more important and involving than writing a diary.

Some of John's letters home have been transcribed chronologically with the diary entries but at the time the mail would have been very slow. Censorship procedures and unreliable delivery across a war torn Europe meant that letters would often take weeks to arrive.

1938 Map of the Mediterranean Region indicating some of the locations referred to in the diary.

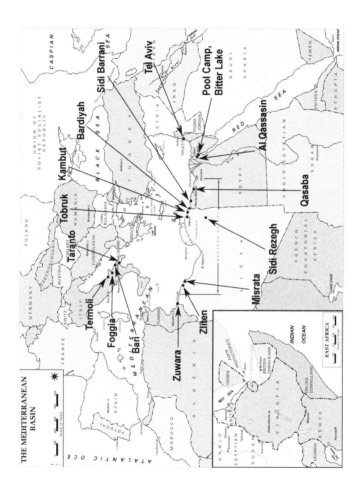

(Picture source: United States Military Academy Department of History)

14

In the Blue - Behind the Front Line

3. THE WAR DIARY - written by John Gill from 1941 to 1945

We had a beautifully peaceful trip of miles. We put in at Freetown, Durban, Aden, Port Sudan and Tewfick. Yes on the whole, I really enjoyed it, my first sea journey. Coming into the tropics as we did of course suddenly, the heat was terrific, but I rather liked that. Eating meals or when below deck we perspired uncomfortably, but it was so very much out of the ordinary, that I didn't mind in the least.

November 1941 - Egypt

After an event-less trip on the sea, we slid into Port Tewfick harbour - the end of the voyage - after nine weeks.

We arrived in Suez harbour, the sun blazing down. What struck me straight away, was the intense dryness. It was quite hard work carrying our kit about. But we perspired very little, unlike the sea voyage, on that we were wringing wet from morning to night. From there we were taken to a "Pool" camp 30 miles from Suez. We were there a week and I grew to like the place very much. It was situated a mile and a half from the estuary of the Suez Canal. This particular place was called the "Bitter Lake" for some unknown reason.

We were allowed down most nights for a bath, and I think that is what made me like the place so much. I used to like to get down there early, have about an hour in the water and stroll back. The sunsets were marvellous, a big red sun illuminating the sky and silhouetting a little knot of palm trees at the side of a stream. Miles of golden sand stretched endlessly into the distance and

16

the hot dry air felt like a warm blanket after the long spell in the warm clear waters.

Well as I said, we were there 7 days and I was rather sorry to be posted. Two recently made friends and I were sent 350 miles west of Alexandria. I arrived on the 5th November 1941, and the weather was extremely hot. We were again quite near the sea, about 2 miles, and went down every Sunday afternoon, which we were allowed after work. By the way, this little place was called Qasaba.

The hot weather was soon over. We knew about it when we got a severe sand storm. Anyone who has not been in a sand storm cannot possibly imagine it. It's the most deadly thing I've ever come across for making a person miserable. The depression it induces is unbelievable, I never felt so miserable in my life as I did in this and other sand storms. After one of these, one invariably gets an attack of "Gipe Guts", as its called out here. It's a severe attack of diarrhoea, and a mild form of dysentery.

It was after a sand storm that a mobile cinema came round, and no one, (who hasn't been stranded in the "Blue") can imagine the relief with which this is welcomed. Just sitting there miles away from the desert hardships (of which there are many I haven't mentioned) it was heaven. I have never enjoyed a show more, and never will again. Two of them came around to us while we were at Qasaba.

Then came the rains. I wouldn't have believed it if I hadn't seen it. The sun scorched sand soaked up hundreds of gallons. But then it couldn't take it, not half of it, and we were flooded out. We had to get out of bed in

17

the middle of the night to dig a trench round the tent, but we couldn't keep it out. We had two or three inches inside, it was grim. In 2 or 3 days it drained away, but then it came again. It came 4 times in four weeks, and every time we were flooded out.

I had been at Qasaba 6 weeks when the first big push in Libya came off. It didn't concern us much at first. I was on an Air Stores Park, and we just supplied the requirements of squadrons. We didn't get many air raids. An odd plane came over one night and dropped 4 or 5 bombs on the outskirts of the camp. And just before we moved up nearer the front, a plane strafed the camp, but no one was hit.

As the troops progressed in Libya, we moved up to an abandoned German camp at a place called Kambut, 35 miles from Tobruk and from Bardiyah and Halfaya. You probably remember Halfaya being in the news - but I'll tell you about that later. I'll give you an account of the trip from Qasaba to Kambut-------

20th November 1941

Dear Mother and all.

I don't know if I told you or not, but I got an air mail post card from Frank -------- on the 12/11/41. It had been sent on 28/10/41 so it only took a fortnight to arrive. That was the first word from Doncaster since I left, and boy! Was it welcome. He assured me all was well at home, and that meant more to me than anything. I suppose you heard the news of the push on the wireless, but that doesn't

18

concern us. So you have no need to worry about me. I am still well, comfortable and happy and still my only worry is you. If you are alright, so am I.

I am getting a lot of experience that I never would have had normally, and am profiting by it. By the time you get this I shall be 20, but if everything goes alright, I shall be with you on my twenty first, at least I sincerely hope so. But time seems to flash past here.

I'm afraid it's a devil of a lot of writing which tells you nothing, but if I can keep assuring you that I'm still well and happy, I think you will be satisfied. In two three months time, we were told, we could tell you about the ship we came over on, and the escort which will interest Frank.

From your loving son, brother and grandson,

John

December 1941 - Libya

We set off on the 23rd December 1941. We made fairly good progress the first day, about 84 miles. Most of that was by road, from Qasaba to Sidi Barrani, and then, owing to the Germans being still in Halfaya, and Bardiyah, had to turn off into the "Blue" and travel by compass. If anyone who reads this has ever done the same, forgive me for mentioning the camping part. In my opinion it's interesting, if not pleasant. At sunset, the convoy was dispersed at a certain spot somewhere south of Sidi Barrani.

We raced for our dinner, only to find that the cooking

trailer had broken done some fifty miles back, and we would have to go without food until it caught us up. We had gone without tiffin *(Note: Old Indian English word meaning lunch)*, and the only meal we had that day was a scanty breakfast. (We had expected hardships but not empty stomachs). Still we could do nothing about it, so we went back to our lorry, put ground sheets on the damp ground curled ourselves up in 5 blankets, and tried to sleep. I have never spent a more uncomfortable night in my life. I had been told previously to coming out here, that one prayed for an English winter, but don't you believe it. All this winter I've been longing for warm weather to come. However, we had a pleasant surprise in the morning, we found that the cooker had caught up with us during the night. We all dashed for breakfast, and got tomato soup dry bread and half a cup of tea. It's a long time since I enjoyed a meal so much.

The rest of the trip was much the same. we had two meals a day, both consisting of bully beef and biscuits. We did get half a mug of warm tea every meal time, but that is the only liquid we saw the whole trip. It lasted 7 long days. Always miles and miles from nowhere, hundreds of miles in the "Blue".

We travelled about a hundred and fifty miles north and then turned west on the third day of our trip. We came to, and went past, many graves of German and Italian soldiers. They had been given a decent burial by our chaps. A bit further up we went through the numerous tank battle fields, and believe me they were numerous. The thousands of tanks that had been put out of action astounded me. At first there seemed to be more British than German. But as we ploughed through the sandstorm that had blown up, we saw hundreds of German and

In the Blue - Behind the Front Line

The battlefield at Sidi Rezegh was part of Operation Crusader which was a military operation during the Second World War by the British Eighth Army against the Axis forces in North Africa between 18 November and 30 December 1941

(Picture source: South African War Museum as published in: Klein, Harry Lt-Col (1946). Springbok Record. Johannesburg: White House. Publication was 63 years ago. In South Africa, copyright prescribes 50 years after publication.)

North Africa Advances of the Axis and Allied Forces 1940-42.

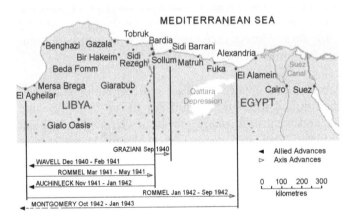

(Picture source: www.anzacday.org.au original Australian Department of Public Information – Army)

21

Italian Panza vehicles that had been either destroyed or damaged. That I think would be Sidi Rezegh, El Adem and all the other places there has been so much said about on the news. We saw a few dead, who hadn't been collected or buried, and everywhere was that same horrible reminder of what had happened two or three weeks earlier.

The material that had been captured lay in immense piles all over the place. It must have been hell on earth while it lasted, and I thank my lucky stars I hadn't been in the Tank Corps.

Well we arrived at this little place between Bardiyah and Tobruk. There were seven very adequate huts the Germans had left, we used them for offices etc. It was quite a treat to eat and work in huts instead of tents. However, apart from benefiting from the huts, we were much worse off here for several reasons. The food was very bad, we had no paraffin, so couldn't have stoves or light lamps. We had several light raids, and the atmosphere was very depressing. The depression, believe it or not, was far worse than any of the other unsettling things. The second day after we arrived a Dornier "Flying Pencil" came over as we were going to tiffin. It circled round two or three times taking what we thought were photographs. We were all watching it, ready to duck, when we saw two bombs leave it. We thought we'd had it. The bombs hit the ground quite close to us and bounced up again, this time landing farther away. So we popped our heads up and watched them. They exploded a few seconds later. The blast shook us. We had begun to think they were 'duds', but soon changed our minds. We've had several over in the day time, none have done any damage, but there a damned nuisance. We had several night raids, bombs all around the camp, but no damage – yet.

There were heaps of rifle ammunition and hand grenades on the camp when we arrived and the armoury chaps have had a real picnic, slinging grenades right and left. It's not very nice for us, but they're having a great time. I needn't mention how bad our nerves are at this time.

12th December 1941

Dear Mother and All

I received Franks card on the 9th, Mary's card on the 10th and a letter and card from Mother on the 11th the very first from home. You can't imagine my feelings, if I'd been a bit younger I'd have cried. I'm certain they were the only things I wanted. They were all sent on the 11th and 3rd of Sept. So you have got a good idea how long they take. The letters brought back memories too, about my sea sickness, we were told it lasted for 4 days, mine lasted more than a week. I wasn't sick, just lousy, but I did enjoy the trip. By the way, it won't do any harm my telling you now, we were convoyed from Blighty by the Repulse, it was a big shock to me to hear that was sunk only days after leaving us, it is surprising how safe we felt with that ship along side us, but, the next time we turn round, it's at the bottom. It's a damn silly world this. It's grand to know you've got some decent people in the house, it's taken a load off my mind. I'm sending another letter tomorrow so until then, Cheerio.

Tons of love
John

The Dornier Do 17, sometimes referred to as the Fliegender Bleistift ("flying pencil"), was a light bomber.

(Picture source: www.anzacday.org.au original Australian Department of Public Information - Army)

HMS Repulse was a Battlecruiser of the Renown class. It was lost in a Japanese air attack on 10th December 1941 off the coast of Malaysia. John would have heard of the sinking on the radio prompting the comment in his letter.

(Source: Photograph A 29069 from the collections of the Imperial War Museums (collection no. 4700-01)

4th January 1942

Dear Mother and All

*I'm afraid I've been rather careless or thought-
less, Mother. I forgot to send your Birthday greetings, I
hope you'll forgive me. But, better late than never I hope
you had a very happy birthday Mother. I can't very well
say more, but it's not the words on paper that count, as
you know, but the thought that I do think about you always, all of you. I am living for the day when I shall be
home with you again. But I am, (as I hope you are), making the best of a bad job, and it can at times be quite
pleasant. As I've said before, it's much worse for you than
it is for me. I had heard before I came out here that one
prayed for an English winter, but don't you believe it, I
shall be very glad when the hot weather comes. At
present it's freezing cold at night, too cold to be comfortable in the daytime. We're getting bags of rain. Even now
I'm writing in my great coat and I started with gloves on,
but couldn't manage it. We had our blu's taken off us, and
were issued with battle dress, and boy! Do we need them,
we wear them day and night.*

*I'm sorry about not sending you any snaps, I in-
tend to, though I can't get hold of a camera. I'm waiting for
the warm season and then I'll bribe someone to lend me
their's. I'll most certainly send some soon. It seems a devil
of a long time since I left Blighty, but actually it's only
about four and a half months. The bottom of the page
comes without noticing, so I'll pack up.*

*Tons of love and best wishes
John*

January 1942 - Retreat

I think it's about 3rd or 4th January 1942.

A spot of good news - Bardiyah fell yesterday. About six thousand eight hundred Italians were captured and over a thousand Germans. About twelve hundred of our troops who had been captured, were released also. It is believed that the reason Bardiyah and Halfaya were so strong, is because they were preparing to strike at us from the rear. Thank god we're getting the better of them, or we would be right in it. Halfaya is a pain in the neck now, but they won't get any more stores in from Bardiyah, so I think it's a matter of time. The holding out of these two places has been a great help to the enemy. Our supplies have to go a hundred miles or so round, and it's holding up our advance at least three or four days.

There are very strong rumours of an enemy offensive coming off, on a big scale in Libya. We naturally hope not, but the rumours are getting more definite.

We get a few bombs on the outskirts of the camp at night, and we're getting "cheesed" off with having to get up. We're getting so used to it that we just stay in bed and hope for the best. I suppose we'll get some on the camp one of these nights.

I must mention our Christmas dinner - it consisted of bully beef stew, some Xmas cake and pudding which was going mouldy with keeping. There were some nuts, but they vanished long before I got to them, a tin of beer too, was welcome. But, the whole dinner wasn't enough to fill a mouse. This is only a trivial thing, I know, but

26

things like that mean a lot to the boys out here. Everyone was very dissatisfied, particularly when they thought of their pals in Blighty who were in the RAF, having a darned good time, and leave into the bargain. They, I suppose will think themselves badly treated because they can't have a fortnight off at Christmas. I wish they'd think of the boys out here occasionally, the majority, I think, are envious of us, seeing sights in foreign countries. It certainly sounds good, but I and many of my friends, have never been off the desert since we got on it, not even to Cairo or Alexandria.

Mid-January...

This offensive scare is materializing. The CO of our unit has been given instructions as to where we will retreat if necessary. What a life! I shall soon be a nervous wreck. The bombing still goes on all around us nearly every night, and now the possibility of retreat.

The enemy in Halfaya thank goodness, packed off the other morning, I think it would be about 15th 16th 17th of January. We had lost count of the time here. Anyway it was a great thing for us, there were more Italians than Germans, perhaps that's why they packed up.

Well the German offensive started. We got some news at four o'clock one night. (I can't remember the dates, and none of my pals know, so I'll have to skip them). We got all packed up that night. Everyone was panicking, but we managed it. When we had finished it we were told to go back to the tent and get the majority of our own kit and get some sleep.

The next morning it had blown over and we were to unpack. We did and forgot all about it. The following Sunday, about a week later, we had walked down to the beach (about 8 miles). We got back at about 6.15 at night and found the panic on again. We were just about dying on our feet after the walk, but we had to get all packed up again. It took us until half past eleven to manage it, and only then with half a bottle of whisky an officer had given us.

We, (or the main party) set off first thing in the morning, in the worst sandstorm I've ever seen. I had to stay behind on rear party, and was very pleased. The sandstorm was deadly, it blew our tent over and it took us about half an hour to get out of it. After that we lived in one of the huts, but still got smothered in sand. We were there three or four days and by that time the majority of equipment had been taken away. We were taken back, (to our old camp at Qasaba) by plane, but the least said about that the better. It was a very old plane belonging to our unit, and one of the struts was broken. I have never been so tossed about so much in my life. At the slightest variation in the atmosphere it went up or came down about 20 feet. I felt pretty sick, but not as bad as most of the boys. Anyway we are back at Qasaba and settling down pretty normal again. In fact 20% are going on leave every week now. I can't rake enough money up at present , so I shall be going the 5th week, that will be 3 weeks from now.

February 1942 - Close Bombing

Well I haven't written a word for about 3 weeks now because there hasn't been a thing to write about. But last night we had several Gerry's over. One dived over the camp several times and then went inland to take a run in.

28

We ducked. The bombs came sizzling down. My knees turned to water, so I just sat in the old trench and waited. There were three. They dropped about 50 yards away, and the shrapnel rained down. Two of my friends were hit, and one of them will be crippled for life, poor devil.

We found our working tent riddled in the morning and our living one with shrapnel strewn round it. One half pound bit was found in the trench in which we were squatting. The tent which our corporal had just come out of had 3 or 4 big holes through it, and a piece of shrapnel had gone through a bed, and that was about 6 yards from our own. That was about 28th February 1942.

March 1942 - First Leave

It is now 4th March and we haven't had any bombs since and I don't suppose we shall.

My leave, I shall be on my way in four days, I shall have £5.10 shillings but I shall manage, and have a good time, but most of the boys get through about £15.

Two days before I was to go on leave, I developed a septic elbow and had to go in "dock". The M.O. told me I would be out in four days, but it turned out to be ten. On the third day of ten we had Gerry over. He or rather they, dropped their bombs all around us. Then the camp machine gun opened up, that brought the devils back. The machine gun nest was about 50 yards from the dugout ward. The two 500 pound bombs he aimed dropped almost on top of the dugout. The bombs were 16 yards apart and my 'hole' was right in the middle of them. It came through without a crack and went down for about seven feet perhaps more and that's a terrific hole in the desert. Where we are the sand is like granite and bombs usually explode on the surface. I think it a miracle our dugout wasn't flattened. The bombs made a terrific noise which lasted (or seemed to), for several minutes. So we have another thing to thank God for, and I do, with all my heart.

Mid March....

After that little episode I finally went on leave. I managed fairly easily on the money I had, and had a very good time. The main form of entertainment, pictures and skating, but we had a really good look round Cairo. The Zoo, Pyramids and Sphinx, Museum, Mosques and numerous parks were exceptionally interesting.

We saw King Farouks Palace, but that was nothing to look at. I had heard quite a lot about the Cairo brothels, so we went to have a look. A lot of the lads say that's how they started going regularly, but I didn't have much difficulty getting out. It did nothing but strengthen my mind against it. They're repulsive places and in my opinion, the boys who go for one reason only, want their heads looking at. That's my opinion but there are thousands who don't agree.

Anyway, our leave was finished. We were told before we set off that the train in front of ours had been bombed, 6 killed and 20 injured. It didn't sound good, but we got back to camp safely to find it had been strafed a couple of times while we were away.

A week later 3 kites came over and started diving over our camp. We thought we'd 'had it'. They kept it up for an hour but didn't drop a thing. We found out the next morning that they were night fighters, our own, you can imagine my feelings. I felt like sending the air ministry a dirty letter.

Two or three nights later we got a warning through on the phone. The planes came over our camp, quite a number of them. They dropped dozens of flares two or three miles away. They gave the unit hell for an hour, but didn't touch us, thank god. I'm doing quite a lot of complaining about the bombs etc. But we were quite well off compared to some of the units.

Well we've had a quiet spell, and I'm enjoying life much more. I go swimming nearly every night. I couldn't swim a stroke before I joined the RAF, but I am getting quite good now. A mobile cinema comes round once a week and it's surprising how it soothes ones mind. I've a couple hobbies too. One is carpentry - more or less. Still, I've done some pretty good work tables and stools. Racks for coats, rifles, gas clothing etc. And the other one is drawing. I never knew I could draw. I'm certainly not very good, but some people think so, and our office is like an art school room. We're just discussing the possibility of making model air planes, not a bad idea. Anyway we're not having a bad time. We have to get up occasionally at nights, a dozen bombs were dropped on the other side of our camp last night. But my spirits have risen quite a lot lately, and it didn't worry me at all. Perhaps I'm getting used to them. I used to panic quite a lot, but it doesn't worry me now.

Life in the desert seems to be getting more pleasant as time goes by. We're getting plenty of fun and sport. We go down to the sea every night, we were down there all afternoon and evening yesterday. I had been on guard the night before and I was certainly ready for some sleep. But it's quite a healthy life, and I don't dislike it half as much as I did.

April 1942 - Flares

It is a month since I wrote that bit, and since then the Germans have been getting rather persistent. They don't worry us much, they just drop flares, circle round for a few minutes and then fly away. Some units round here have been bombed, but we have been lucky up to now. We have had flares directly over head twice, but no bombs. It certainly keeps your nerves in a knot until the flares go out. It seems much lighter than day while they're on. I wouldn't worry if I was in a town but in a small camp like this it seems - to us - that it is unlikely for us not to be hit.

May 1942 - Third Push Starts

The THIRD push has started up here. Actually it started last week, about 30th April. The Germans started it, but I hope - and it seems - that we're finishing it. I hope with all my heart that we go right through this time. Tripoli none stop, boy! That'll be a smashing piece of news. It's rather doubtful, the weather is much to hot for tank battles etc. Its bad enough in winter, but this weather, I should say it's almost impossible.

June 1942 - Retreat to Ismalia

Well that was about a month ago, I have changed my opinion since then. Tank battles have been fought and apparently efficiently too - on the side of the Gerries. I

32

have more experience of retreats and panics etc. The order to pack and get out came one tiffin time. The Gerries were then 25 miles from Marsa Matruh, we were 16 miles on the other side. Anyway we left Qasaba the day after we got the order, and the Gerries moved in next day. It took us almost 2 days to do 200 miles, the traffic on the road was amazing. I had no idea we had as many vehicles in the middle east, and these were only on the western desert. There was one continual stream the whole way from Qasaba to Alexandria, with hardly a break. That was just coming down, the stuff going up was nothing in comparison. In fact it annoyed me considerably to see these hundreds and hundreds of vehicles coming down and so very little going up. Still they probably know what there doing, but considering what a mess has been made of things up there, I doubt it. Although we're hardly in a position to criticise.

Well we landed up at a place called Amaria, plenty of trees around, which was heavenly. We stayed there about 3 weeks and then started packing again. Boy! was I cheesed off with packing and unpacking. But this time we only moved about 5 miles into the Blue. We seem to be doomed for a rough time. As we expected, we were on our way again within a fortnight. (I'll not pass any remarks on my feelings, they're not the sort to be spoken about).

As it turned out, this was a much better move. It was about 250 miles from Amaria, we went through Cairo, and I had my second glimpse of that famous city. My spirits recovered. We went to a place about 20 miles the Cairo side of Ismalia. There were 3 cinemas within reach. But the biggest attraction was the shower. We had a shower hut almost on the camp. A first I used it 3 times a day, but the novelty soon wore off, and went every night. But after having so little water for so long, it was wonderful to be able to wallow in it.

Half day trips were organised for us to Ismalia, and it is a very pleasant little town. I enjoyed them very much. We went swimming (for which I have acquired a great passion, although not very good at it) and then went a stroll round the shops. Just looking in shop windows seems a childish pastime, but when one hasn't done it for six or seven months, it gives great pleasure. We went to the French Gardens, it is a park similar to some we have in Blighty, and I (who have a good share of imagination) used to lie on the grass under the trees and imagine I was back home. The only snag with that is, it gives you a nasty jolt when you come back to earth.

We then went for a tuck-in in the Garden Club, a very pleasant little place right in the middle of the garden. They dish out unusually good food. Then the only thing left to do was to go to the pictures. Ismalia is a very dull place at night, but they had open air pictures which are very pleasant, except for mosquitoes. Then make for home, its funny we call our scruffy little tent "Home" but it seems quite natural because we have made it reasonably comfortable. Primitive furniture and I at least have made a very good bed, which makes a terrific difference. Although always subconsciously homesick, I am very comfortable (considering some poor devils. Not necessarily round here, but in the desert.)

After a few weeks we were given the chance of seven days leave. Everyone jumped at it, but I had no money, these half day trips have seen to that, but, as always with me, a miracle happened. My Flt/Lt, who is an extremely good chap and likes me, (I think more than a little), offered to lend me the money. I borrowed £10. That may seem much to much for a week, but then you have never been to Palestine. One can, and some do, spend £20 to £30, some even more, but I won't tell you what on or who they spend it on. But Palestine is much more free of the muck and slime of these Egyptian towns. The people are Jews, and if anyone believes all the bad things that are said of them, they can take it from me, they're wrong. Some are all, and more, that is said of them, but so are some of our own people. I've met all types, and as far as I can see, all nations differ a great deal, but in there own way, Palestinians or Jews are as good a race, and very similar to English.

My friends, (the two chaps I met on the day I was called up and have been with them ever since), had an extremely good time. We saw a great deal of the old biblical place around Jerusalem. Actually we stayed in Tel-Aviv, but went on trips to Bethlehem etc. I won't put down all the things we saw, it would take to much time, and wouldn't interest you much. It is enough to say we had a very good time, and were very sorry to leave. When we got back (this is an example of our efficiency) we had moved from one side of the road to the other. To make room, I think for the army. But the army didn't come. So we are now eating in tents instead of huts, with a very good camp site empty over the road.

17th August 1942

Dear Mother and All

Hello everyone. I have two quite pleasant things to tell you. I've been on a sudden seven days leave to

Palestine. For my leave I went to Tel Aviv, I can't tell you much about it in this airgram but I'll write a long letter straight away. We went to Jerusalem also and saw all the places mentioned in the bible. I'm certainly adding to my small store of knowledge. I think I shall go to Palestine for my next leave, it's a very pleasant and interesting place.

Cheerio, lots of love - bags of it.
Your loving son, brother and grandson
P.s. How are you getting on Grandad? Ok I hope.

John

1st September 1942
My Dear Mother and All

I hope you don't mind reading junk, because this is another one of 'em'. I haven't a scrap of news to put in, well, perhaps just a scrap. We heard just a few minutes ago that things were moving up the line. But no one knows where, why, how or in what direction. So it's not much use mentioning it, you most certainly will know more about it than me. Anyway don't let it worry you, and remember what I told you.

How are things in Doncaster? The mail is pretty bad at the moment. Yesterday and the day before I received five papers and Illustrated, for which I thank you. But apart from that, I have had nothing of importance for almost three weeks. I know your not to blame for that, there must be dozens on the way. I'll probably get a big pile all at once. The whole units in the same boat, so I'm not worrying.

Cheerio, God bless, lots of love, all the best and all the

36

rest (joke)

From your loving son, brother and grandson.
John

September 1942 - Boredom

The date is now 16/09/1942 and there is very little do-ing. We're still at Qassassim and getting "cheesed off". All on the camp would like to get back to the desert, and I really believe I would too. This site was alright at first - the showers, pictures, trips into Ismalia, (but we don't get the trips now), and the novelty of showers and pic-tures has worn off. Although I still like the pictures very much, and go there almost every night.

But at Qasaba we had a cinema show once a week, and enjoyed it much more than we do now, everyday. Still we are comfortable and safe, so in times like these there isn't much more we could ask for.

11th October 1942

My Darling Mother xxxx

This (as you only too well know) is the second Christmas I've been away. But don't forget the old saying (3rd time pays for all) and if I'm home this time next Christmas, it will certainly pay!

A Merry Xmas means all I can possibly say, so God bless you mother.
John

October 1942 - Drunk in Cairo

The date is 15/10/1942

Three weeks ago I re-mustered to MT Mechanic, I got well under way with my training and, as far too often in the RAF, was moved to the Sergeants Mess. Two men are sick, and there is a shortage of ACHs *{Note: ACH was an abbreviation for Aircrafthand, a low skilled post involving general duties}*. If the Sgts. would pull there weight, one of us could quite easily manage. But of course, they must have their cup of tea in bed and be waited on hand and foot. I'm getting really fed up with the job. They must have the best of everything, if it's not quite up to scratch they moan like hell, (or like babies). It's going to shake some of them when they get back into civvies, and have to work, it'll be very unusual for many, believe me!

I'm still in the mess and still smouldering. One of the chaps should be coming back soon and perhaps I'll be able to settle down again.

The two men, by the way, have got Malaria of which there is quite a lot about just now. There are about 20 men down on our camp, and there are only 200 or less, in all.

I've just put in a pass for 24 hours, to Cairo on Monday, (it's now Thursday), and that may break the monotony a little...

We had a very good time in Cairo, I'm afraid we got a little drunk, but it's not a frequent occurrence, so it can, I hope, be excused. My friends insisted on a celebration for our 1st anniversary, - we celebrated alright. First of

38

all we went to the pictures, it was a little late when we came out, so we went straight to a hotel and had 3 double and 2 single whiskies in 20 minutes, stupid? You can't tell me it's stupid. I can't be chastised enough for it, but at times (when you've been away from civilization for a long time) you're not in your right senses, and go absolutely berserk. When you find yourself right in the thick of it, that's how I feel, it's amusing how the noise of traffic confuses you. I've stood in the middle of some crossroads in Cairo, and not known which way to turn, you feel right in the middle of something much too big and confusing for comprehension. I don't suppose you understand me, but if you've spent twelve months in the middle of the noiseless and endless desert, you will.

Anyway, to get back to the point, my friends were much older and more experienced in drinking than I but I still had to show them the way home and put them to bed. I surprise myself at times. I never have done much drinking, but have occasionally been drunk and I have always been able to act and talk almost normally, and never loose my senses. I don't know if that's an asset or not, sometimes I'm pleased, sometimes I'm annoyed. The fact remains, we had a good time. We were in a dream the whole of the next day, but we considered it worth it.

November 1942 - Successful Offensive

Three weeks later. On the 1st November to be precise, just about twelve months since I arrived on 31 ASP. We started an offensive out here, and boy what an offensive. The first few days Baltimore, Boston Mitchell and Kitty bombers made a thousand sorties a day. They (I think all of them) went over our camp 18 at a time, continuously. The Kitty bombers took off from a drome next to our camp, to act as escort. So I know how many there were. They were taking off, landing, fuelling and loading up and taking off again. At one time the Italians asked for an armistice to bury their dead, it must have been hell for those poor devils, but, I suppose they are the fortunes of war we keep hearing about.

Anyway its now the 5th November the exact day I joined this unit and the Germans are in full retreat. (I haven't mentioned the army because I know nothing of there doings, except that they are making a bigger effort than ever before, but anything that may come from this offensive may, I think, be put to the credit of the RAF. I am certainly proud to be one of them, after watching the show they put up.

We got this "gen" from somewhere, and I think the source reliable, we captured 9000 prisoners, put out of action 270 tanks, shot down 300 planes (they may have been destroyed on the ground, I am not quite sure), captured (or put out of action) 300 odd guns.

Those of course are not all, we've seen Italian lorries come down the road already, the gains this time must be enormous. I'm hoping against hope that we can drive them right out of N. Africa this time and by the look of things, its by no means impossible. Still, that remains to be seen.

We (31 ASP) have naturally moved up towards the front, at present we are at Amaria, but are expecting, at any time, the order to advance again. Now on the 5th Nov the Germans are still retreating, somewhere this side of Marsa Matruh that is where this unit was before. We will be back "home" at Qasaba any time at all Yim Kim maybe.

Now on the 16th Nov. We are still at Amaria the Germans have been pushed back to (or almost) to Derna. 72 thousand prisoners have been taken, mostly Germans. And we, as I have said are still here, I don't know why, we've never been as far back as this in an offensive but it suits me, I've seen enough of the Kambut area.

December 1942 - Driving

Well, I'm afraid I spoke to soon, now, on 12/12/1942 we are well passed Tobruk, near Bomba. We left Amaria on 29th Nov (2 days after my 21st birthday). It was another rush affair. We were given orders on 28th in the morning, and half the camp was away in the afternoon. I went the following day driving an ambulance, for the very first time. I had a pretty good idea of how to drive, but I have never been on the road, and they actually asked me to drive a five-day convoy. Naturally I accepted for the sake of experience, but had I known the state of the vehicle I would have point-blank refused. But, I accepted and drove 460 odd miles. There were some very steep hills with dangerous precipices, but I made it, the gears were awkward and there was a lot of play in the steering. But to my intense relief we arrived at our destination on the fifth day, all in one piece.

The story is precisely the same as the last trip to Kambut, tons of enemy material, thousands of prisoners, but no air activity from him whatsoever, and for that, I am more than thankful. Our present site is not good, thousands of mosquitoes, and gallons of water, (that sounds queer), but I mean rain, it rains almost ceaselessly.

And now, on the 22nd of Dec it is almost Christmas, we have made one or two preparations, sports have been organised for Christmas day, and I have entered into nearly all the events, boxing included. I prefer wrestling to boxing, but I think I can put up a pretty good show. I really intend to enjoy myself this Christmas, to make up for what I (or we) missed the last time. I feel as if the Christmas spirit has entered into me already, I feel strangely excited and full of beans. I suppose we miss so much out here, that we're inclined to get childish over the least provocation. Anyway I'm happy, it doesn't matter a damn if its childish or not, as long as that's a fact. My only worry in the world is that my folks at home and myself, of course, are happy and safe. That perhaps sounds selfish, but I am intoxicated with the spirit of Christmas, forgive me. Now I suppose the only thing that really matters is the successful conclusion of this war, my life, and even perhaps, the life of my family, is very insignificant at the side of that fact.

January 1943 - Another Journey

1/1/1943

I won my boxing bout easily, in fact, I felt very sorry for my opponent, it was only a three round affair, but he finished up with a very sore eye, and a very bloody nose. I hadn't a scratch and finished with plenty of wind. In the afternoon, we had racing, I came second in the main one, winning 10/-. Then dinner, boy!, what a dinner the finest I've had since I left home. We were served by the officers, and its surprising how much good humour there can be among a crowd of chaps, even on a battlefield. We had a good time, got almost drunk into the bargain, but that's beside the point.

42

18th Jan 1943

We left At-Tamimi on Sunday 3rd Jan and I was not sorry. I had seen enough of that place, but when we were on the road I began to change my mind. When I set off we were given a tin of bully and a packet of biscuits to last us three days (or rather three tiffins) on the second day it rained and oh! how it rained. I was driving an open Ford, I tried all ways to block out the rain and freezing wind, but, it was no good, I got wet through and frozen to the marrow. At night, we pulled in near an old Italian fort, the ground was 6 inches deep in mud, dozens of the lorries got stuck. I managed to get through, but I was lucky. At night we had what little food there was for us, and tried to find a warm and dry place to sleep. Nobody did. I slept in the cab, as I said it was an open one. I tried to block it up, but the wind was too strong. I gave up, put my ground sheet over me (which blew off umpteen times) and tried to sleep - I didn't.

It was the same all next day but we were more fortunate at night. We pulled in near some Italian buildings, and went to a lot of trouble getting our beds in.

That trip was a test of endurance for me, but I suppose that is another thing we have to put up with in war. We are not really badly off, but I'm thankful its not worse.

This place is Sidi Magnum, (I don't know how it is spelt, but that's how its pronounced) and its not too bad. We can get no Naafi stuff and rations are short, but apart from that, were okay.

Sunday 31st January 1943

We have been here almost a month now and we have just received orders to move again. We move off on Tuesday. This time I am quite pleased, it means an uncomfortable journey of about 500 miles. But we are going in the direction of Misrata just into civilization again. It's about 120 miles off Tripoli. So we should be alright for 24 hours leave if they approve it, which (I suppose) is doubtful. This will be our longest move and I'm driving again. I'm not so pleased about that, it's a bit of a strain driving on these roads in convoy, and we'll be lucky to do it in 6 days...

Well, here we are again, just the Tripoli side of Misrata, it's quite pleasant too. Plenty of palm trees and a town within walking distance. Actually it's 5 Kilometres, but we have walked it twice already.

There are very few civilians left, but it's nice to get into a town again.

The trip here, by the way, was almost an enjoyable one, the weather was good, which was the main thing.

30th January 1943

Dear Mother and All

Hello folks, I've been listening to Goebbels speech *(Hitlers birthday you know). A Palestinian translated bits of it for us. It was an impressive speech, but a bit defeatist, (at least I thought so) "backs to the wall stuff, either fight or die", I believe he said. We've certainly got 'em' worried, they're 100% on the defensive now, and it's our turn to get rough. But I suppose you talk, eat and sleep with war on your minds, so I'll shut up.*

It's about 7 o'clock just now, I'm trying to picture what you will be doing at home this minute. But, the house has (or must have) changed so much since I left, that it's almost an impossibility. I can imagine Mary dashing round, getting ready for a dance. And you Mother, always the same working like the clappers at your sewing machine. And Grandad "listening in" intently sucking on an empty pipe. I suppose it will be empty quite a lot lately eh! Grandad. I wish there was something I could do about it, but it's the same here at the moment. We can get absolutely nothing in the way of canteen supplies. I've just used my last bit of soap, don't know what I'm doing tomorrow. But it's not always like this, usually we are much better off than you folks. If the mail was coming in normally I should be as happy as it's possible to be. I shall never be 100% happy in this mob, but no-one ever is, so why worry? The only things we have to worry about are monotony and boredom, so obviously we have nothing to worry about. I think I'll go to bed early again tonight, I'm sleeping like a dead 'un' lately. I've got to be treated with brute force every morning or I'd miss my breakfast. Good job we have some early risers in the tent, or I'd miss it every morning. I always was a darned nuisance at home, remember?

Love to all,
John xxxxx

February 1943 - Moved Again

9th February 1943

Just as we are settled down again we have received orders to pack, we are moving about 30 miles up the road, away from Misrata to a place called Zliten, the most holy place in N. Africa. But not a place for us. The people are very anti British. While we were there we had a very good time, apart from canteen stock which was nil.

Sports were well organized, and I really enjoyed the month we had there.

Food was very bad the first two weeks but we made plenty of complaints, and it improved. We had some very bad weather at first too, but that also improved.

As I said, we were a month, and we had to pack again. I was not very pleased this time being put back on the ambulance, but it was very useful for sleeping in at night. We had plenty of rain etc. this time, but my vehicle was much more water proof than on the last trip. So it turned out alright. The trouble is that I cant get used to the Albian gears and it hurts my vanity to grate them, which on that I can't avoid.

27th February 1943

Dear Mother and All

Just received two letters, the 2nd and 27th November, and the 10/- from you Mother. I appreciate you doing these things Mother but shall I tell you how much money I have on me at present, £7. I've never had so much money in my life, so although I love you for it Mother, please don't send any more. I have £15 to £20 in credit and my Act. M.T.M has just come through so I'm really in the money.
You'll have to excuse the writing, I've broken my pen nib, this is one I've borrowed.
Well nothing of any interest has happened lately, so I have very little to tell you. Except, perhaps I'm

playing football more than I've ever played in my life. And I'm getting quite good at it, I've become one of our teams goal scores (on a mild scale).
We are having a lecture on Tripolitania tonight so I'll get up there.

Cheerio, lots and lots of love,
John

March 1943 - The Illness Begins

We arrived at our destination, Zuwara, on the third day and a bunch of boils started to appear on my neck and face. I must have been in a very poor condition, for about 10 o'clock the following morning, I began to feel an acute pain in my side, and it was getting steadily worse. I went to sick bay several times, but the medical orderlies didn't understand it. So I was told to grin and bear it and they would take me over to a nearby 'drome to see an M.O. *{Note: Medical Officer}* the following morning. Well, I can't explain what sort of night I had, I was delirious most of the time, the pain was getting damn bad. The next morning I could hardly walk with it. The M.O. obviously didn't understand it, but my temperature was very high. So he sent me in dock with multiple boils, I was annoyed about that, the boils didn't mean a thing now.

I had a nightmarish trip to the nearest hospital, it was 40 miles away, across a very bumpy sand track. I died a thousand deaths at every bump, no-one is more surprised than I that I didn't collapse when I got out. I was really in a bad state, I got into bed with a hell of a great sigh, but the pain didn't ease up any. It hurt like the devil

47

every time I breathed. I was examined almost at once, but he still didn't find the cause of the trouble. He left me alone that night but I still got no sleep.

Two M.O.s came in the morning and gave me a really good going over. They found I had pneumonia in the left lobar.

April 1943 - Getting Better?

From then on it was easier, still had lots of pain, but it began to ease up. In 3 weeks, (7th April 1943) I felt a great deal better, but the mobile hospital was on the move, so I was evacuated to Tripoli, that's where I am now, 24 MRS *{Note: Medical Receiving Station}*. and doing fine. Still got a slight pain, but there's a really good M.O. here, and I think I'll be out and about in a few days.

That's what I thought, pains kept cropping up every-where in my right side too. So I was back on M and B tablets *{Note: M&B, May and Baker or 693 tablets were names given to the antibiotic medicine sulphapyridine}* and was quite annoyed. I had 4 days of continual sickness. I'm on the last day now, they're taking me off M and B tomorrow, and am I pleased. They really made me ill this time. It's the 19th April.

22nd April and feeling fine again. Slight pains still in my chest and got a bit of a head cold, but apart from that I'm normal except for being darned thin. I've got a massive appetite so I hope to fatten up soon, Still in bed but I think I'll be up soon.

28th April. Yes, at last I'm up, for an hour today perhaps more tomorrow. This morning the M.O. said he'd
send me down to base for a holiday, boy! Am I hoping.
That's just what I need, about 2 months doing nothing,
(I don't, but it'll still be great,) catch up on the swimming etc.

I hope I go to a rest camp where there's a gymnasium,
that's still one of my passions for some reason or other.
If I was fit and got into a gymnasium I should go crack-
ers. And there's nothing I want more at the moment
than to be fit. I'm sick of moping about in bed.

> 25th June 1943
> I received a letter card from you today, the first
> in ages. I also received one from Auntie Belton, but I'll
> answer that if I have time - when I've finished this.
> Your letter is dated May 8th Mother. No !! I don't
> think you're a child, and I'm sorry about the rosy pictures,
> or - as you will call them little white lies. But when I found
> out they'd sent you a telegram "seriously ill" I was a little
> annoyed. It seemed to me unnecessary, and I tried to
> smooth it over a bit. If that is being seriously ill, then it's
> not to bad. Certainly I had a rough time for a bit. But now
> it's all over, it doesn't seem much. The worst part of it was
> the first fortnight. I just couldn't get rid of the sand as the
> tent was in a bad position, and the wind blew right through
> it, blowing up the sand. I wasn't too good there either, but
> that first fortnight was the worst. When I was sent to
> Tripoli I was ok. What spoilt my stay there was the fact
> that they put me back on M and B tablets and I was very -
> oh! - very sick. When I got into Cairo, here I still seemed
> ok. That abscess, by the way, was what I think they called
> a lung abscess, it was just in the right place for draining
> too. Apparently, if it had been in any other place they
> would have had to hang me upside down some how or

other. So it wasn't too bad, had a bit of a temperature and a nasty cough, very, very little pain. Now I'm feeling 100%. But it looks as if your not going to believe me when I tell you I'm fine. I wish you would Mother, because it's really true. I've been swimming today and got really sore with the sun. My grammar's deadly.

There are three chaps in here, and they just found out they're going home, and have been celebrating, they're really "blind drunk" and lord! what a noise.

By the way, why is Len going to Durban, you didn't say in your letter, is it through his illness? It is very doubtful that I shall follow him, I think I am destined for a life of leisure in Cairo.

I'm not much thinner, Mother but perhaps I do look older. That seems natural enough eh! as I am 2 years older than I was when I left.

Frank's getting around a bit isn't he? He should get a glimpse of London from there.

You say you're longing to hear I am on convalescence leave, I'm as good as on. I leave next Tuesday 29th. I don't know how long I shall be there, or what happens when I get back. But the thing that matters is that I'm going. I'm going to Tel Aviv, of course, as I said in my other letter.

Well, I also am running dry, it seems to take me all my time to write 3 pages now, but I'll soon come up to scratch.

Cheerio Love,
Your painfully affectionate son John xxxxx

July 1943 - Convalescence, Tel Aviv

It is now the 10th July 1943

I was sent down to base alright, it was a lovely hospital,

food, treatment and beds, could not have been better. I had been down at RAF hospital a week when my temperature started playing tricks again. It was hovering around 100-102 for a fortnight. I had umpteen x-rays, Wing Commanders and god knows what checking up on me. They were all very interested. Apparently these cases don't come along every day. I had one more x-ray on about the 14th day, and my trouble was solved. Out of about 10 x-rays only this one showed the lung abscess. It seems that this is a fairly serious business, because every M.O. that has seen my papers since, has whistled or looked surprised, and asked me how my chest is. But I felt no pain, in fact I was quite annoyed with having to stay in bed, if I was seen to move quickly in bed, I was told off. That lasted perhaps 5 or 6 weeks and I didn't notice it much we got such perfect treatment. The strange part of it was that I slept very well every night and felt almost normal. Occasionally my temperature was so high that I became delirious, and for perhaps 3 or 4 days I lost my appetite. The worst complaint was my cough, it was a horrible one. I felt as if I was dragging my socks up, and it kept bubbling in my chest. It almost made me sick once or twice. And the stuff I brought up when it burst. It smelt horrible and looked the same. But that's enough of dirty details. They let me get up very gradually half an hour, 1 hour, 2 hours and so on until I was up all day. I went out into Cairo one day.

I had a lump on my leg for 2 months and when I walked around it swelled up. I told the M.O. he had it x-rayed, and, damn it, it was another abscess. I was told to rest!!! After 3 months in bed!!! I was told to lay on my bed all day, dressed. I've never felt so impatient in all my life.

Anyway, despite this abscess, I was sent on convalescence to Tel Aviv, that's where I am at the moment, and quite fit. My leg has gone down, my chest feels almost perfect. I still get occasional pains, but nothing to worry about.

I'm leading a life of luxury, the food here is lousy, but I've saved plenty of money during my illness, so that can be overcome.

I go swimming all day and ever day which, of course is very good for my lungs. I'm getting quite good too.

We were in a small café last night, there were 4 Yankies in, my friend and I, and a girl and her father over the counter. The girl was very young and the man very old. The drunken Yankies kept asking for more drinks, it was after time, so she couldn't give them any. They kept on asking and the girl got annoyed and told them off. The Yanks didn't mind too much, this being a girl, but my pal, also being a bit drunk, tried to be chivalrous and get the Yanks out. They of course didn't like it. There was a very big guy, much broader than me and very aggressive, he came over and was going to (and could have done easily) wipe the floor with us. The 4 Yanks were all round us, and very drunk. If a fight had started, I think we could have said goodbye, they were certainly tough guys. Many times they were on the point of socking us, but, although it took an hour, we calmed them down without bloodshed. I don't know how it was done, because they were in a hell of a mood. Anyway, we all left great pals, or so we have to suppose. My opinion of Yankies has gone still lower. They had about 4 gin and limes (we were watching them) and they were ready to fight anyone, particularly Englishmen. That's what I don't like about them they're too proud of themselves, they think they're winning the war and are as tough as hell.

23rd July 1943

Dear Mother

> *Just taking this opportunity of telling you that my leave is ended, and that I am quite normal again (and that's the truth, I really am fit). I should be swimming twice every day, and I'm burnt almost black by the sun.*
> *I suppose I have to go back to the hospital for a final check up, anyway I think they'll find me A1. You need have no fear about my health, so you can switch your worries to Frank, because I know you must worry about someone, and Frank needs moral support more than me. I imagine he does anyway.*
> *I read one of your letters yesterday, 5th July, but I'll answer it when I get back. I'm all packed and ready to move now. I'll write again soon, Mother.*

> *God bless you. Your ever loving son John xxxxx*

24th July 1943

My very best Mother

> *I received 2 of your letter cards yesterday 22nd and 28th June. I'm very relieved to hear that you have had news of my recovery, and I assure you, it has been a complete recovery. I feel absolutely normal, I'm swimming and lazing on the beach all day, and I'm more brown than I've ever been in my life, which is saying something. A horrible dirty blackish brown, and I'm very fit eating enough for 6 men, and getting plenty of exercise. I really don't think that they'll send me home, Mother I probably*

have been rather ill, but I've made such a perfect recovery that it wouldn't help much to send me home. I hope that doesn't sound as if I don't want to come home, I want nothing as much as that.

I'm sorry about Frank, I have assumed that he's in this Sicilian affair, but who knows? It's going really well over there anyway. I think he'll be quite pleased, I believe he wanted to see a bit of the world on the quiet.

Yes, the M.O. told me I was lucky with the abscess, it was in the best possible position for draining, and everything went according to plan. They were all surprised at the speed at which I improved.

You make me proud to be your Son, Mother, when I hear of the pleasure you experienced when you received the good news.

I'm becoming a terrible letter writer. I'm getting too much pleasure lately and it's putting me off.

I'm getting a few of your letters now, but I have dozens to collect somewhere, they'll be the ones that were sent to 31 ASP. Because I think I've had all those sent to "RAF Hospital".

You say some of the chaps of the 8th Army who have been here a long time are home on leave. Do you know what the army mean by a "long time"? Well there limit of overseas service is 7 years, ours is 4, so that'll give you some idea. Some of those chaps have done over 4 years now, I've done nearly 2.

I'm not trying to disappoint you Mother, I'm just not as optimistic as you in the matter.
My brains gone quite numb so I'll go for a swim now and see what I can think up when I come back – Bye!

Well I had a lovely swim, trouble is I was in the water about 3 hours and left it too late to finish this. It is now of course 15th July. I've got just 6 more days at this place, and then go back to hospital, that's just to check up on me I suppose. We went to the pictures last night, for a reasonably modern town, this has some lousy cinemas.

But we found a decent one last night.

The Sicily jobs going well eh! I'm listening to all the news with impatience, and wondering if Frank really is in it. I can't think where else he can be though, if he isn't there.

I'm sorry about the writing Mother, but this ink I'm using is like soup and it runs when it feels like it. I'm just getting ready to go swimming again, it's a great life, swimming all day. I'd better pack up now. Cheerio Mother and don't worry about Frank, he can take care of himself better than me and I'm doing alright.

Your overwhelmingly affectionate son John

Ps. I still keep forgetting to put the numbers on these letters, I'm sorry.
This ones 33rd

6th August 1943

Dear Mother

I've just had a beautifully riotous afternoon. I thought I had received most of my mail, but just after tiffin today someone brought in 25 letters and one paper (December 24th). I didn't know where to begin. I got them all in order of the dates (most of them were April, May and June) and what a pile they seemed. It took me a good two and a half hours to read them. Among them were one of Franks, 4th Nov 1942 and a Christmas card of yours 18th November and one of Mary's, early January. It isn't much use answering those.

I'm just beginning to realize what a shock those fateful telegrams were to you. I'm awfully sorry Mother, but at the time I didn't worry about myself in the least. It never entered my head that I may be seriously ill. I

certainly didn't feel as ill as I must have been, although I
felt pretty ropey. And I really am not worthy to be the
cause of so much worry. I feel quite ashamed of myself. I
gnash my teeth every time I think of those telegrams.

Well, you've pleaded with me so many times in
those letters to "come clean" and give you all the "gen",
that I'd never be able to look you in the face again if I
didn't. So here goes, you know all there is to know about
my condition except one thing, and you may even know
that by now because I told Mary in my last letter to her.

When I first got into hospital I noticed a lump in
my leg, just like an ordinary bruise. That's what I thought it
was, and thought no more about it. It didn't go away like a
bruise though, and when 2 or 3 months later, I got on my
feet and walked around a bit, it began to swell up. I told
the M.O. and he promptly had it xrayed. It was another
small abscess. They thought it might go away without
treatment, so sent me on my Convalescence leave. Well it
stayed down (fortunately) for my three weeks , and came
up in earnest as soon as I got back. That's why I'm still in
'dock'. They cut it about a week ago and it's doing fine.

So, here I am and here I stay for another week
or so. Goodness knows what happens then, I'll probably
go back to Tel Aviv again, I hope so. It's going to be a rude
awakening when I got back to work after 4 such lazy
months. I didn't tell you about my leg for the obvious
reason Mother, I know what a glutton you are for worry.
I'm sorry if you think I'm not being fair to you, but you just
put yourself in my place. Apart from that I can assure you
I'm really fit and well, (same old story uh?) but it's quite
true this time.

You are right about getting the best treatment
possible, expense is not even considered, i.e I've had
about 15 xrays in all, and that is only one example. It's
probably a blessing that I'm in the RAF at this time, but
that's a stupid thing to say if I hadn't been in the RAF I
wouldn't have come out here, and if I hadn't come out

here I would not have had pneumonia, etc. It was the conditions out here that did it. I'm certain I don't think the climate would affect me, I rather like it.

I seem to have neglected you quite a lot when I first went in 'dock', Mother. My mail to you seems to have been deplorably scarce, I'm sorry, you must have had a devil of a time. I'm glad you received that hanky though, I was rather proud of that. I'm afraid I haven't received those photos of home yet, but on looking at the dates of some of these letters, there's still hope.

Reading these letters though, you seem to have been in doubt as to my condition, for weeks and weeks. My idea of smoothing things over has made things a good deal worse. I kept saying "getting up tomorrow" (which was, on more than one occasion, quite true), and then you got the official notice, and didn't quite know where you were. Never mind love, it's all over now. I don't think anything will happen to me now for a bit.

I'm very happy just now Mother, for no particular reason, unless it's the arrival of all that long lost mail. That certainly was a relief, I was hoping those snaps were among it, but no luck. I'm getting used to this lazy life, getting quite good at it in fact.

I'm just listening to 'Happydrome' on the wireless and just can't concentrate, if you read a lot of tripe, blame the wireless.

I'll pack up now mother before I tell you all about 'Enock'.

Your very affectionate son John xxxxxxxxxxxxxxx

7th August 1943

Dear Mother

I had a colossal afternoon yesterday. I received all my back mail all at once, 25 letters and 1 paper. I sent you a long letter last night so this is just to tell you in advance. I'm afraid those snaps of yours weren't among them, but I haven't given up yet.
We've just had a concert here in the hospital, by the way it was rather good. We used to get a film show twice a week, but haven't seen one for some time now.

You are probably wondering why I'm still in dock, that letter will tell you all about it when you get it. I've had a small lump on my leg for about 4 months now. Well it just swelled up into another abscess. Nothing to worry about though, I shall probably be going back to Tel Aviv again, which of course suits me.

Well so long for now.

Your very affectionate son John xxxxxxxxxx

7th September 1943

Dear Mother

I am now at Transit camp waiting to be posted back to my unit. I am quite happy about it so you have no need to worry on that account. I am perfectly fit. It's a bit of a knock coming slap bang on to the desert after the luxury of the RAF hospital, but I don't really mind now I'm fit. I think for about another month you had better use the above address, they will reach me more quickly, because I shall be here some time yet. In many ways I'm quite pleased to be going back there, I know all the chaps and they will be in some decent country from now on. They are either in Scicily or at Cape Bon so that will suit me. I'm quite looking forward to the trip, but the stay here isn't

58

going to be so hot. Transit camps never are luxurious
places. Cheerio for now love, and remember, I'm FIT!! I'll
write again tomorrow.

Your loving son John. xxxxxx

13th July 1943

Still in Tel Aviv convalescence camp and 100% fit, I'm
really up to scratch now. I'm as brown as a native, in
fact browner than most. Honestly I've been pretty brown
before, but never as bad as this. I'm almost black.
Everyone on this camp goes down to the beach, but I
haven't seen one as brown as me yet. Apart from this
swimming etc. This life is very dull, at night all there is
to do is go to the pictures, walk on the prom or sit in a
café drinking. Mostly I go to the pictures.

September 1943 - PoWs & PTCs

After 3 weeks my convalescence leave finished, I had
had a good time, but wasn't sorry to leave. As soon as I
got back to the hospital, my leg came up worse than
ever, it was very painful too. I was stuck in a bed again,
what a life. The abscess was cut while I was under a
general anaesthetic. It healed up OK in about 5 weeks,
during which I was kept in bed. I am now, I think OK, at
least, I hope so. I don't feel quite up to scratch but I
suppose that's quite natural after 5 and a half months in
dock. I came down yesterday to 22 PTC *{Note: Personnel
Transit Camp}* to wait for transport back to my unit, and
what a hell of a place this is. As I said, I came down
yesterday, and have been put on guard all ready. I go on
at 5:45 tonight and am I cheesed! - Just come off guard.

59

10/09/1943

I go on again this afternoon, what a racket, it's only for 3 hours though. When we came off we heard some glorious news. Italy has surrendered, boy, am I happy! I want, more than ever now, to go back to my unit, I'll see Italy perhaps.

I wasn't keen to go back to "31" but now we are in decent country I would be stupid to refuse. I think if I had applied, I could have got a base posting (I almost did do too). But in Italy, food should be better and conditions all round should be much better.

And so, to Italy!! Let's Go!

I hope Germany realises that she's beaten, pretty quick. I want to get out of this mob as soon as possible, this isn't my idea of life. I'm a peaceful sort of chap, there's nothing I want more than to get back in my rut at No "91". It is funny how as a lengthy absence from home increases, so does ones love for it. Even though the memory of it becomes fainter, home as a house and furniture, doesn't mean a thing. It is just because it is home and contains the only people you really love. That it becomes the only place worthwhile. ------ (All this after a guard, I've become all sentimental and poetic). I don't think it's the guard that's done it, its the good news.

Home has become considerably nearer.

I wish I had gone into more detail in this trashy diary of mine - but perhaps I will re-write it some day (I shall have to before I dare show it to anyone else).

September 10th 1943

More good news, we have just heard this morning that Mussolini has been handed over to the Allies and is now in N. Africa. I am wondering what we shall do with him, but then, I have a good idea, we shall treat him like a king and give him 90% freedom. Prisoners of war (we have a good many on this camp now) are treated with more respect than we are, that really is a fact. This PoW camp is more comfortable and pleasant than any camp I have been on myself. They have an easy, comfortable life, a lot of them say openly that they do not want to go back to Italy just yet. I don't mind prisoners having a good time, but I do object to them having a better time than us. Still the fact that they are prisoners and away from home, makes them entitled to a little pleasure; I suppose.

13th September 1943

Monday and touched for guard again, this is a racket. 24 hours 2 on and 4 off - I'll go skats! There is a concert in Cairo with Jack Benny, Larry Adler etc. Free, tomorrow night, that, I suppose, is why I'm on guard, - fate, I suppose.

15th September 1943

Things certainly work fast around here. I was on guard all night and had done 4 hours guard on the Italian prisoners in the morning. I was relieved at 10:45 (it should have been 9:30). At 12 o'clock I was at the station all set for Alex. *{Note: Alexandria}*. What a hectic hour and a quarter! Sweat was streaming off me. I had to hand in my blanket to get my clearance certificate signed up, and pack, and what crowned it was that I had to collect my laundry that I had handed in a day earlier. It wasn't ironed, so got everyone dashing around and they ironed it whilst I waited. It took them a good 20 minutes. When I got to the lorry it was just moving off. I had been scrubbed off the list, anyway, he put me back on it again, and here I am again another PTC, horrible places. I'm just trying to get off onto Alex. I've had one go, but I was 5 minutes early so he sent me back, the B-!*!

16th September 1943

Well I eventually got out into Alexandria. I went to the fleet club, which by the way is about the best club in the middle east. I went to the pictures, became very "cheesed", and came back. Nothing exciting has happened today, I've done 2 hours PT *{Note: Physical Training}* which has me (literally, and almost actually) on my knees, I then went swimming and am now "on my caps badge", as the saying goes. Still I think I shall go to the beach this afternoon, (haven't enough ackers *{Note: slang for £s}* to go to Alex). I shall laze around in the sand all afternoon, it's a better occupation than most.

17th September 1943

On guard again last night, but I don't think I shall get another one for perhaps a fortnight, if I'm here that long. I hope not.

25th September 1943

And I'm in one hell of a bad mood, for apparently no reason, unless it's because my face is coming up again in sceptic spots and small boils. Nothing annoys me more than to have my face peppered in spots, which is beginning to occur quite frequently. When this happens I'm troubled with acute self-consciousness, and, I suppose, a slight persecution mania. Anyone who looks at me longer than a normal glance, I feel like smashing his face in and nothing would please me more than a good scrap. It's very stupid I know, because my face isn't really too bad, but although I realise it's stupid, it doesn't help my feelings and I feel as tough as hell. After a recent close combat course, I feel that I could hold my own with any man, or two (I'll have to try it some time). Nothing, of course has happened since the 18th. I saw "Gone with the Wind" yesterday, for the first time, my friend thought it was a lousy film, but he's hopelessly dim, actually it was a beautiful film, the story, the acting and the scenery were superb. I had read the book, of course, so I could appreciate it more. The scenes were almost exactly as I had pictured them. Anyone who is genuinely bored with that film cannot appreciate art, and I feel sorry for anyone who cannot appreciate art and beauty. Afterwards, we went to a cabaret. Which soon displaced the pleasant atmosphere the film had left around me. We had a lousy night, (I felt slightly sick at the sight of these horrors calling themselves girls, who are there for the sole purpose of conniving drinks from love-starved desert-rat stooges). I felt rather tired, so came back to my flea trap of a bed. I couldn't face the fleas last night, so took my blanket outside and woke up this morning wringing wet with dew. Still it was worth it, I got a very good nights sleep.

I seem to be able to write better when I'm annoyed. I'll have to get really angry some time and see what I can do. I'm just going for tiffin, and then will go for a swim, it's the best remedy I know for ailments whether physical or mental... Just come back from the swim, I had the most enjoyable afternoon I've had for a long time. I can stay in the water, swimming, for at least half an hour now, which, for me is no small achievement. I am also learning a lot more about diving. I'd like to be able to show Frank a thing or two when we get back. I shall have to put some hard work in though if I intend to do that.

October 1943 - Hospital Again

4th October 1943

A bit more progress with my swimming, I swam about three quarters of a mile yesterday. We've now got our eyes glued on the other side of the bay. It is at least a mile across, I intend to do it one of these days.

5th October 1943

On fire picket {Note: a soldier or small unit of soldiers maintaining a fire watch} the last 24 hours. I'll be coming off in 2 hours.

8th Oct 1943

I swam over the mile mark yesterday, easily, with a bit more practise I think I could do 3 miles. I'm rather amazed at myself, some chaps here, who have been swimming all their lives can't (or daren't) swim to the raft. I don't swim as easily as I should like yet. I have not had enough experience to breath quite normally, and it's surprising how much difference that makes.

21st October 1943

I have just realised that this is my friends birthday. I'm rather sorry I missed writing to him, but my memory, I'm afraid, has never been good and it seems to be deteriorating.

Well we are now at sea again, for the second time in my life. At the moment we are about a days run out of Tripoli, I've said that backwards because we are heading for Tripoli.

We left Alexandria 4 days ago in convoy of about 30 ships. We have been crawling along at about 7 knots for 4 days, and it's getting slightly !* monotonous. It is perhaps a ship of 2 thousand tons and there's very little room for troops, but I suppose we can stick it for another 24 hours. She was rolling quite a lot yesterday, but, thank god I wasn't sea sick, in fact I have felt fine this trip.

I should have said this before the description of the trip. We were on the baggage party for this trip, which means there were about 400 or 500 chaps coming from Aboukir {Note: Abu Qir} transit camp to this ship. We collected all their deep sea kit, brought it to the ship and put it in the hold, about 24 hours before we sailed. We did that alright, but we had to wait for the old transfer tub coming in. It was about 11 o'clock at night when we finished, then we had a ride of 15 miles back to camp. That's what must have caused all the trouble. We had had no food all day and could get none back at camp, so we went to bed without. I think, between 12 o'clock and morning I was sick 30 times (or hardly sick with an empty stomach) just heaving - heaving. I couldn't remember having felt so ill in my life. By the time I had finished I hadn't the strength to get out of bed. I just laid there and heaved, what a night, and what a condition to start a sea voyage. God knows how I found the strength to get up and get on the lorry that took us to the docks. What must have caused that, I think, was the ride in the open lorry at night and with my shirt open. Still I got over it slowly, and am now, on the 5th day feeling fine.

It is now the 24th Oct. and we are still a days run out of Tripoli. For some very peculiar reason we cut off for Malta after we had passed North of Benghazi, for the life of me, I can't think why. We dropped no men and no material there, we were just anchored in the harbour for about 12 hours. If all goes according to plan this time we shall be in Tripoli harbour tomorrow morning. I sincerely hope so, already we have made an 8 day run out of what should have taken 4.

31st October 1943

Our calculations were slightly out, we arrived in Tripoli at about 5 o'clock in the evening. We stayed on board that night, and disembarked at 10 the next morning. 39 PTC was 10 miles west of Tripoli, not a bad place, an old Italian fort, plenty of trees etc. around. We got there at 11, and I was in bed in sick bay at 4, septic cyst on my face, I had a beautiful face for about 4 days. It's like home coming here, my second time, of course. Don't I have some great luck? I'm doing alright now though, face has gone down to almost normal. I shall be out very soon, I hope, I don't want to miss my posting over the water. I'm very anxious to get out of this country now, cheesed off with this infernal sand.

The fact that I'm back in hospital again after 6 months of it, is very annoying. I don't really mind when I'm in for a good reason, but there is very little wrong with me, and I feel like a malingerer! Being an up-patient in an RAF hospital is the very devil. Once you get up (at 6 o'clock) your bed is taboo, if you are caught sitting or laying on it after it has been made, you are literally pounded on. One has to sit on a small stool all day and read, or walk round the garden, which will cover just 12 square yards in this case. There is a recreation room somewhere, but I have never succeeded in finding it. Things could be worse, I suppose, food is good, and I have a good bed, but the thing that annoys me is the fact that I'm in here for no (or very little) reason, and I may be missing my posting over to my unit. I should be really annoyed if I didn't go now.

I was in there exactly 7 days, seven unnecessary days. My face just went down on its own, and I was sent back to 39 PCT which was just moving back to about 5 miles east of Tripoli. My! How we worked in that move, tent striking and loading until my back ached and my hands blistered.

We were at the new site 2 days and were packed off to the docks again. Italy none stop! But what a voyage that turned out to be. I've never been so cold, uncomfortable, tired or hungry for so long in my life. Firstly we had to sleep on deck, right up in the bows where there wasn't a scrap of shelter, (I had scrounged 2 blankets, but what are two blankets on a deck in a rough sea?). It wasn't particularly rough, but we were in a tank landing craft, a flat bottomed effort, and she rolled so much that we all thought the next one would tip us right over. The spray kept coming over wetting our blankets through - it will take me a long time to forget that trip. I wasn't sick, which is strange, I didn't even feel sick which is stranger. It was still a horrible trip. I couldn't sleep and needless to say we got bully and biscuits for every meal. The trip lasted 5 days. It was certainly a memorable trip!!

We arrived in Taranto harbour on the 5th day (yesterday) 12th November we wandered round Taranto for a couple of hours, and pushed off for Bari straight away. Bari is on the east coast and rather a nice city. It is much better than Taranto, we are about 5 miles outside it at the moment (13th Nov) expecting word to push off for our units. The sooner I get there the better I shall be pleased, the worst part of it is that I haven't the faintest idea where "31" is yet.

4th November 1943

Dear Mother

I have very little room to write as you can see, but these few words convey all my feelings which written, are far too inadequate, so I'll just say:-

Xmas Greetings.
All my love and God bless you mother.
John xxxxx

4th November 1943

Dear Grandad

It's not often I mention you in my letters nowadays, but believe me, I haven't forgotten you. Cheerio, and I hope next Xmas will be a happier one.

Lots of love John xxxxx

December 1943 - Italy, a good Christmas

4th December 1943

I have been back on 31 almost a month now. We left Bari by the way, on the 14th Nov and came straight up by rail to Foggia. The sight of Foggia shook me, they tell me it was partisan bombed for 24 hours and I believe it. It was in a hell of a mess. The railway was one mass of twisted metal (the goods yards at least). The town too was very badly knocked about as bad as some of our worst towns in Blighty. We stayed outside Foggia for the night in an army transit camp. We were kicked out of the transit camp in the morning and stuck on a railway dray. I still hadn't the faintest idea where my unit was, but fortunately I saw the name of one of the stations "Orta Nova" that was where I had been led to believe my unit was, about 7 miles out. I walked it with all my kit. I arrived on "31" several hours later in a devil of a sweat, but the greetings I received outweighed my fatigue. Everyone thought I had gone home. The unit is just the same as ever, we get very few canteen supplies, but food is reasonably good and plentiful. We had a cinema show last night. We have been into Foggia twice to see ENSA

69

{Note: Entertainments National Service Association} shows, and on the whole we have nothing to grumble about. I'm very happy to be back at my job and feel more confident than ever since I came back. I have done valve grinding, de-carbonizing and mostly big jobs. I'm feeling much more important and now I've done them, much more confident.

6th December 1943

Nothing of importance has happened. Working on a transfer case for 2 days and learned all about 4 wheel drive (a subject which has, to me, in the past, been very vague).

7th December 1943

Extensive preparations are being made for Christmas on the camp just now. A pretty big stage has been rigged up and a reasonably good band has been discovered among the boys, we have plenty of really good talent too. It's a pity we don't organise more concerts, we certainly have the facilities here. We should have plenty of beers and almost too much wine.

We have turkeys and pigs, plenty of fruit - yes, this promises to be my best Christmas in the service.

Thursday 9th Dec 1943

Still nothing to report, preparations still going full blast for Xmas. Still working enthusiastically. On guard last night.

13th December

Cinema show tonight, Abbot and Costello in "Pardon my Sarong" should be good.

January 1944 - Quiet Time

9th January 1944

Christmas, of course is over. It was nothing to get hysterical about, but not on the whole, bad. We had a very good concert and lots of wine, but by now, I have a strong dislike for Italian wine. That's about all Xmas amounted to, the Xmas dinner was not bad.

Unfortunately I have neglected my duty in writing this diary. I am rather annoyed about that, because however insignificant it may seem at the time it always seems interesting a few years after. It is now, I'm afraid.

12th February 1944

Dear Mother

I'm afraid I still haven't got a decent pen, but hope you can read this lot. I wrote you a letter card last night, but I think you'll have some difficulty in reading it.

I started telling you of my adventure. I may as well carry on, it well help to fill up. I told you, if you can read it, of the time I was in the middle of 2 bombs 15 yards apart and of my tent being riddled with shrapnel. Well another time, I actually saw him drop his bombs. We were going to tiffin at the time and a flying pencil came over very low. We didn't realize it was jerry at first, until he had circled round once. Then he dropped 2 bombs. I saw them leave the plane and he seemed right over head.

They landed about 300 yards away, and I saw them bounce among a cloud of sand. There was nowhere to hide so I just watched them. Stupidity! They didn't hurt anyone.

All this happened a very long time ago and actually I've nearly forgotten about it, but you asked for it and here it is.

I was in Tripoli hospital (just I was sent down to base) when a bomb ripped a corner out of the building.

All this looks very exiting and all that, but I can assure you, we thought very little of it at the time. It's all in a days work, and I'm not in the least touchy about these things.

There are dozens of small insignificant things which would look impressive on paper but, don't mean a thing in real life. I think I've done far too much line-shooting for one letter. If my pals knew I was telling you this they would laugh at me. But my excuse is, you asked for it!!

It was when you told me Bill had been a 100 yards from a bomb that made me put that stupid remark in, about telling you of some of my "adventures".

I would have told you before, of course, but I know how much you worry about these things, and there really was no need to worry. A near miss is as good as a mile away, I can assure you. Those few incidents didn't effect me in the least and spread over a period of two and a half years, they didn't occur very often. Also I haven't seen a jerry 'kite' for over a year now, so there is very little chance of there happening again, (or I wouldn't have told you about them).

I'll have to pack up now mother, so cheerio, and don't start worrying about these little things.

From your loving, but I'm afraid slightly secretive son,
John xxxxxxx
Hope you don't mind me keeping these things back.

April 1944 - Jankers

9th April - still 1944!!!

Nothing of any note has happened since I last wrote, except that - I lost my tunic, wallet and paybook (for which I did 3 day jankers *{Note: Jankers or Restrictions of Privileges is an official punishment for a minor breach of discipline}*).

The unit has again been moved, we are now just behind Campo Marino near Termoli, and I have just come back from 7 days leave in Bari.

I was almost drunk twice, we had lots of fun chasing girls (that's all we did do, chase them). We went to the pictures once or twice and saw a performance of the "Merry Widow" straight out from Blighty. On the whole had a reasonably good time, but I still don't think any more of Italy, the people or the country.

May 1944 - Dentist

17th May 1944

I've neglected my diary again, trouble is, there's nothing of interest happening just now. I hear Casino has been taken, but nothing definite.

The dentist has been round the camp and mine have been classed grade 3. Up to now I've had 2 big ones filled and one out. I've two more to get out, I've been 4 times already.

22nd May 1944

Taken up boxing once again, feeling very fit. Getting plenty of cinema shows on camp just now. Last night we had "Take a Letter Darling" best show I've seen for some time. The chaps in the tent are talking about wo-men and I'm cheesed. Goodnight. Just finished the book.

{Note: A literal statement that he had in fact used up all the space in the little note book he was using to write his diary}

{Note: Despite the September 1943 armistice between Italy and the Allies, German forces implemented plans to occupy the Italian peninsula. However, following the fall of Rome in June 1944 the Italian campaign became of secondary importance to both sides. It wasn't until nearly a year later on 2nd May 1945 that German armed forces in Italy were forced to make an unconditional surrender to the Allies.

Throughout this period John was stationed in Italy but no diary has been found for this period, perhaps he didn't consider it worth mentioning but more likely the diary has been lost. The following entry "My Trip HOME!" was found in another completely separate note but no further war time entries were found. There are a few faded photographs of his time in the latter stages of the war indicating that he was able to enjoy some of the sights of Venice and other places around the country before returning home... So, maybe he was just too busy}

August/September 1945 - My Trip HOME!

After 4 long and weary years I was worried about the state of my mind. I didn't feel half so elated as I should have felt. I had pictured myself dithering with excite-ment - completely out of control. But instead I felt nor-mal, in fact extremely bored at the usual very slow progress of the RAF organisation. Probably a very normal reaction.

We first went to Bari, I and five others, on the 3rd August 1945. We were there just a week and were beginning to get optimistic because one of our party was working in the orders room. He was getting all the gen for us. I was leaving in a Lancaster bomber in 2 days time, he even gave me the number of the "kite". This was naturally much too good to be true. So, I was sent to Naples to wait for a ship, - was I cheesed. Anyway we got to Naples and heard favourable reports, so I cheered up a little. But, after a week despair set in. Chaps were coming in and going out the next day, also flying home, and we, about twenty of us by now, had to wait for a ship. We had been overseas much longer than the majority of the others too. We marched up to the C.O.'s office a couple of times in revolt, but he managed to pacify us. God knows how, it very nearly turned into a fight. Still, eventually we did leave, and the C.O. breathed a great sigh of relief. We had been there a month!

The trip took us 9 days of very hard work for me, spud peeling. We worked all day and every day in nothing but shorts. Couldn't wear shoes, there was too much water about - ankle deep. But, we were getting nearer home, so we smiled and told them to do there worse. At this stage, we didn't care.

We stopped at Algiers and Gibraltar and arrived in England on a Friday, 11th September 1945.

There was a band on the pier and I felt a lump in my throat at the sight of Liverpool. I'd never before had reason to love Liverpool, but just then, I loved Liverpool like my mother.

The next morning before it was light we were off the ship and into some lorries that were waiting, no customs procedure or anything. They took us to the station where we piled into the first carriages. An officer came round with some tea - every one howled. We were dished out with chocolate and fags and then went to Morecambe to be put into civvy billets, we left for home in about 3 days. Not bad organisation for once!

The home coming was the happiest and most peculiar happening. Mary, by some sort of intuition, was there, and I just stood and looked - speechless. I didn't know if I was coming or going, I didn't know what to say to Mary. I had my kit to look after, a taxi to fetch, there was someone piling my kit in, and me getting into the wrong side. We arrived home, Mother was waiting to pounce on me from behind the door, with tears of joy, for once, in her eyes. It was a momentous occasion and one which I shall never forget. But the day I get out of this mob *{Note: the RAF}* will be almost as happy.

In the Blue - Behind the Front Line

Epilogue

Returning from the war in 1945 meant that John's travel adventures ended, he would not travel abroad again until the 1990s when, with wife Betty, he twice visited their daughter who was living and working with her Italian partner in Venice, Italy.

John was soon demobbed and lived an ordinary life, working initially for the Nuttal family business, famous for their Mintoes sweets. He was a driver delivering Nutall's Mintoes around the country to many places he previously visited as a driver's mate before the war. In 1947 John married Elizabeth Joan Crawshaw, a local girl from Penistone Street, Doncaster not far from his own home. Elizabeth was known throughout her life as "Betty", she was one of 11 siblings (two adopted) four of whom died before adulthood. Betty never knew her parents, both passing away when she was far too young to remember them. Her father never recovered from the effects of mustard gas attacks in the WW1 trenches and her mother contracted Tuberculosis. Betty was raised by her elder sisters in the tiny "two-up two-down" terrace house. How they coped can only be imagined, but it was not an uncommon story for the time. She and John had much in common, including their place of work.

John and Betty had two children, Linda born in 1948 and Christopher 18 months later in 1950. In the mid-1950s they moved to Intake, Doncaster to manage a newsagents shop which by then was one of two owned by his brother Frank and his wife Joan. John continued in this work until his retirement at the age of 62. He and Betty lived out their lives on the edge of Intake in sight of the Doncaster Royal Infirmary.

These diaries were kept by John's mother and it is doubtful that he ever expected them to be read. He never mentioned them to his children, and they were only saved by his sister Mary after his mother's death.

John passed away in July 2004. Shortly after his death Mary passed the diaries to Christopher. He never read them, feeling it was an unwanted intrusion into his father's life. But, many years later Linda's curiosity caused her to ask to read them and the contents suggest, certainly at the outset, that it was John's intention to share his record of events. Although his thoughts may have changed over time it is still an interesting story, if only to friends and relatives. So, during 2015-2016 Linda transcribed them and here we have the brief history of one man's war written by his own hand (with a few background notes added by his Chris).

In the Blue - Behind the Front Line

Lightning Source UK Ltd.
Milton Keynes UK
UKHW02f0939110118
315939UK00009B/215/P